The Curse of a Good Name

`I0418104`

Patrick D. Coats

PDC Publishing
366 Grampian Highlands Drive
ST Johns, FL 32259

First originally published by PDC Publishing 2025

ISBN 979-8-9923104-0-5 (Paperback)
ISBN 979-8-9923104-1-2 (Hardcover)
ISBN 979-8-9923104-2-9 (Digital)

Printed in the United States of America

Dedication

Growing up as a '70s baby, I experienced a pivotal time in American history—on the heels of the Civil Rights movement, a period of change and great hope

for black and brown people. Like many other young black men, I grew up without my biological father, Ronald Ferguson, whom I only met once at the age of eight. However, it was God's plan for my maternal grandfather to take me in at just two months old and shape my life into the man I am today.

My grandfather was the late Dr. Joseph C. Coats, Sr. What a blessing it was as he was a prominent Baptist Minister who transformed a small Church plant of roughly 40 members and, under his leadership, became a thriving mega-church of about 5,000 members during the peak of his ministry in Miami Florida.

He retired in 1997 after 30 years of faithful service at Glendale Baptist Church in Miami, FL. So strong was his legacy across the nation that more than two decades after his passing, at the mention of his name, people from that era still speak well of him and long for the days of his leadership.

I have often felt a connection to the story of Moses, who, as a baby, was placed in a basket in the river near the Egyptian Pharoah's sister's home. She took Moses in, and he became family.

He was used by God in the history of ancient Israel to deliver them from bondage in the story of the Exodus. Similarly, my grandfather took me in and gave me all he had—most importantly, his name. It is a name and legacy that I have been proud of, and I have made it my mission to honor it throughout my life. God has seen fit to call me to the gospel ministry, and His hand of favor has been on my life. I believe all of this is connected.

And in honor of the faithfulness of my late grandfather, I am also blessed to have a fantastic wife, Archalena Coats, and three loving children, Patrick II (PJ), Joy, and Faith. While I feel very blessed to bear a good name, it has come with its challenges, but I have learned that God's grace is sufficient in all things. I dedicate this book to my late grandfather, Dr. Joseph C. Coats, to my wonderful bride of more than thirty-one years, and three incredible children, but also to my deceased friend, James Melton, Jr., and paternal big brother Dr. John Isham Payne Jr., who has encouraged me to share my story with the world.

Foreword

Reverend Patrick D. Coats is a generational man of faith whose life work is to spread the true and living word of God. His courage and unwavering belief in his purpose, paired with his extensive biblical knowledge, grants him unique indisputable abilities to motivate, counsel, encourage, pastor, and touch lives in a transformative way. I have come to know him as a master communicator, both verbally and nonverbally. Fortified with the spirit of God and a deep love for his savior, Jesus Christ, the visual sermons gained from observing the way he lives his life are louder than the audible sermons he delivers. His message and contagious spirit resonate deep in your mind, and heart long after his presence is no longer nearby.

The Curse of a Good Name is Reverend Patrick D. Coats freshman offering to the world and is sure to inspire, enlighten, and inform! This book provides eye-opening spiritual context about the power of a name and is a delicate constructed fabric of storytelling infused with biblical knowledge, serving as the glue that holds the entire book together.

This book has no limitation of genre and provides major takeaways for all walks of life. A one-of-a-kind body of work that is sure to bless all who reads it! A must-have in your spiritual kit bag!

~DR. JOHN I. PAYNE JR., author,
You May Not Be Who You Think You Are!

Table of Contents

Introduction

There's an exciting family dynamic often overlooked, and that is the profound power of a name. One evening, while reclining in bed and scrolling through my Hulu app, I noticed that the famous multiplatinum recording artist Janet Jackson had filmed her documentary. Instead of allowing her story to be told in death, she decided to tell her own story, in her own words, from her own point of view. Intrigued, I watched this documentary. The more I watched, the more taken I was by her story. Episode by episode, I became more enthralled with her journey. By the time I reached the final installment, I had an epiphany: **her story is my story.**

Janet grew up in a celebrated family, the Jacksons—a self-made musical powerhouse.

Her father, Joe Jackson, came from humble beginnings but envisioned elevating his family through music.

The rest is history: you have the Jackson 5 and the most famous Jackson of them all, Michael, affectionately known even after his passing as the King of Pop.

The Jackson name is known worldwide; one could argue that no other musical family has had a greater impact on global culture and pop music.

In the documentary, we see Janet—the baby of the Jackson clan—navigating her teenage years, determined to find her own identity. She recorded successful albums that expressed her journey to freedom and self-discovery, like *Control* (1986) and *That's the Way Love Goes* (1993).

She also candidly shared the blessings and the painful struggles of life as a Jackson.

While watching this series, something else major was happening worldwide. It was reported on every news outlet that Queen Elizabeth II died at the tender age of 96 years old. Affectionately known as Elizabeth Alexandra Mary Windsor. She was thrust into service as a young lady when her father, King George VI, died. She lived an extraordinary life. Immediately following the shock of the passing of this great Queen of Britain and the preparation for funeral arrangements, the public conversation shifted to the family she left behind.

Not even laid in her final resting place, the narrative turned into various interests in the lives of the family she left behind. How will Charles, her eldest son, who is now King Charles's monarch, rule? What will become of William and Harry, his sons? Of course, outsiders can't fully know the personal trials or true emotional landscape within such famous families. It stands to reason that these children of nobility and prestige live extraordinarily blessed lives, enjoying immense wealth, fame, and a sterling family name.

But, one doesn't have to look hard to notice the visible pain and pressure that comes with their famous family name.

While my family name is in no way on the same level as these most prestigious people, I can relate to the pain that comes with a "good name." We often admire and celebrate people who bear names of fame, influence, and high esteem. Some even wish to be them.

But a seldom-told side of this story is the darker reality of bearing a revered name—and the burden of forging one's own identity within it.

A name is bestowed upon you at birth. You do not get a say or vote on the matter. Likewise, we do not get to choose our family. Other real examples are those who are born into a *"bad"* name. For example, no one names their children Judas, after the one who betrayed Jesus. Indeed, a name can be associated with negative life experiences, leading to shame or embarrassment.

How, then, does one overcome a name that carries such a burden?

This book aspires to share the blessing and the curse of a good name from my personal journey, along with several practical biblical principles, in the hope that someone somewhere might be encouraged to overcome the difficult life pressures a name may bring and chart their own victorious life story. There is a blessing and hope in the fact that God almighty knows who we really are.

One of my favorite biblical passages is when God affirmed young Jeremiah, His prophet, to ancient Israel with this declaration: "I knew you before I formed you in your mother's womb..." Jeremiah 1:5.

It is very possible to survive and thrive while discovering true purpose and fulfillment in life—by discovering that you are far more than just a name.

CHAPTER ONE

My Story

> ### *A Journey Through Legacy and Pressure:*
> ### *Growing up as a "Coats"*

I was born into an intersection of generations—the bridge between baby boomers and millennials. My father, Ronald Ferguson, and my mother, Kathy Coats, were young when I entered this world. Their brief relationship never developed into anything lasting. My father was married at the time but separated from his wife; hence, my parents' connection did not endure. At birth, I was given my maternal family name, *Coats*, a name that carried a legacy far larger than I could have imagined as a child.

I grew up in the household of my grandfather, the renowned Dr. Joseph C. Coats, Sr., a prominent Baptist minister well-respected throughout Florida and beyond.

He was a trailblazer—the first African American pastor in Florida to join the all-white Southern Baptist Convention in the late 1960s.

His reputation was built not only on his powerful preaching but also on his extraordinary ability to remember everyone he met. Dr. Coats never forgot a face or a name; this gift made him beloved by all, regardless of ethnicity or background.

There is one amazing story about my grandfather that perfectly captures the impact of his name and legacy.

At his funeral in 2002, two local pastors from Miami, Dr. Tommy Watson and Emmet O. Ray, shared their memories of his profound friendship, integrity, and character. Dr. Ray recounted that if a news report showed my grandfather robbing a bank—complete with camera footage of him holding a bag of money—he still wouldn't believe it. No!

He'd assume my grandfather was helping the real thief turn themselves in. That's the kind of man my grandfather was, and that was the legacy attached to the name Coats—a name I was expected to live up to.

Growing Up Under the Spotlight

Being raised in the home of such a revered figure came with blessings and challenges. Everyone in the community knew my grandfather, and by extension, they knew me. At school, church, and even the local neighborhood store, I was constantly under scrutiny. There was always a feeling that "spies" were watching the Coats clan. A simple childhood misstep might elicit comments like, "I'm going to tell your grandfather," or "You know better than that, you're a Coats child." The pressure to be perfect was unrelenting, leaving little room for me just to be a kid.

Despite the weight of these expectations, there was immense love in our household. As the ninth child in a large family, I was welcomed as more than a grandson—I was treated like a son by my grandparents, aunts, and uncles. My aunt, only a year and a half younger than me, felt more like a sister.

Until I was about six or seven years old, I didn't even realize Kathy Coats was my biological mother.

To me, my grandparents were my parents. They loved me deeply and raised me as one of their own.

Joy, Loss, and Cementing My Place

Our family was close-knit but not without hardship. The death of my Uncle Paul in a car crash in the early 1980s was a painful moment for all of us. Yet, even in grief, our family drew closer.

That tragedy solidified my place in the Coats family and deepened my bond with my grandfather, who continued to lead and love us through life's challenges.

However, life as a "Coats" wasn't without its unique struggles. For example, during my elementary school years, a church minister who worked as the school custodian took it upon himself to be the self-appointed "Coats-children police" and enforcer. Anytime I misbehaved—even for minor infractions like cutting in the lunch line—I'd be sent to him.

He would threaten me with discipline as though it was his responsibility to keep me in line for my grandparents' sake. While well-intentioned, these experiences and many others robbed me of the chance to simply enjoy being a child.

Moments of Defiance and Understanding

A Picture Says A Thousand Words

One vivid memory highlights the pressure we all felt. During a family portrait for my grandfather's pastor appreciation service, my younger aunt—the baby of the family—rebelled. She intentionally frowned for the photo, a quiet act of defiance against the constant expectation to be perfect. That moment spoke volumes about the unspoken weight we all carried as Coats children.

As I grew older, I began to navigate these pressures more effectively. My uncle Joe, a national wrestling champion and my de facto big brother, became a key figure in my life. Whenever I got in trouble at school, the principal would call my grandfather, who would send Uncle Joe to deal with me. Uncle Joe wouldn't even ask for my side of the story; he'd immediately assume the wrestling stance, ready to "correct" me. His tough love and discipline were his way of helping me navigate the high standards of our family.

Another turning point came through the kindness of Deacon Paul Robinson, a church member who noticed the strain I was under. He would often pull me aside and say, "Hey man, don't worry about all of that. Just be a kid. I see you. They're only trying to love you, don't take it so seriously." His supportive words helped me understand that, while the expectations were real, so was the love behind them.

Ministry, Marriage, and a New Chapter

At the age of 11, I surrendered my life to Christ, a decision that anchored me as I stepped into young adulthood. During my teenage years, I became deeply involved in ministry, forming a Christian rap group called L.I.F.E. (Living in the Father's Eyes).

For seven years, we traveled to churches and venues, using gospel rap to share the message of Christ.

Looking back, I can see how God was preparing me for the call to pastoral ministry later on. Through that ministry, I connected with my wife, Archalena.

After years of friendship, serving together in our church's youth group, we started dating. At that time, I was only 21 years old, and we got married at 23. Archalena also came from a family led by a grandfather who was a pastor. Her story mirrored mine, with both of us growing up under the blessings and pressures of ministry life.

Although I was still running from the call to ministry, I couldn't deny that God was at work in my life. The legacy of my grandfather—the name **"Coats"**—was something I couldn't escape, and it shaped my path in ways I was only beginning to understand.

Continuing the Legacy

Marrying Archalena was a major event for our church community at that time. I remember the fellowship hall being packed with people; the church family poured out their love and support, showering us with gifts and prayers.

It was a profound reminder of the benefits of carrying a name like "Coats," a name that connects us to a legacy of faith, unity, and support.   As we began our life together, the weight of the name shifted. It became less about meeting expectations and more about embracing the responsibility of passing on a legacy of faith, love, and service to the next generation. Through every blessing and challenge, I have come to see the name "Coats" not just as a burden or a curse, but as a **calling**—one I am honored to carry forward.

CHAPTER TWO

What's in a Name

> *"A good name is to be chosen rather than great riches,*
> *loving favor rather than silver and gold."*
> *– Proverbs 22:1(NKJV)*

Names matter. They are more than a combination of letters or a simple means of identification. In many ways, a name carries the weight of identity, legacy, and destiny. When a name is spoken, it invokes expectations, emotions, and even memories. Throughout history and scripture, names have carried profound significance, reflecting the essence of a person or their role in God's unfolding plan.

The scriptures are filled with examples of names connected to purpose. Abram became Abraham, meaning "father of a multitude," when God established His covenant with him. Jacob, known as the "deceiver," became Israel, "one who struggles with God," after wrestling with the angel of the Lord all night and receiving a blessing. These transformations signified a shift in identity, a new purpose, and an unfolding destiny.

When Grandma Calls!

When I was a young boy, we would play in the street. Every sport under the sun—football, basketball, roller skating, bike riding, and many others—captured our attention and energy.

I couldn't wait to finish school, drop my book bag, and run outside to meet my friends who lived just down the street. We would play until the sun went down or until our parents— particularly my grandmother—would holler my name, telling me it was time to come home for dinner.

When she called, it was a distinct sound. Even before hearing my name, I knew her voice—it was familiar, the voice of my family. My friends recognized it too. On days when she called and they heard her, they would say, "Pat, your grandmother's calling you. It's time for you to go home."

The way she said my name told me whether I was in trouble or if she was simply sending a routine message. If she said, "Pat, come home," I knew it was just the usual evening call.

But if she said, "Patrick Demetric Coats," I knew I was in for it. It's fascinating how something as simple as a name is woven into the core fabric of who we are—our identity.

The Power of Meaning

Names have meanings. In the Bible, names often reflect the circumstances of a person's birth or the aspirations of their parents. For example, Sarah means "laughter" because she laughed at the idea of bearing a son in her old age. Moses, drawn from the water, received a name that foreshadowed his role in delivering the Israelites from Egypt.

This principle here isn't confined to ancient times. In many cultures, names are still chosen with intention and care, often reflecting values, hopes, or familial connections. Even if some names today seem random—perhaps inspired by a famous athlete, entertainer, or something in nature—they still carry meaning. A name can bring pain or carry burdens; it can be a source of pride or a reminder of shame.

For instance, a child named after a beloved relative might feel the weight of living up to that legacy, while another saddled with a name linked to scandal may struggle to rise above its connotations.

For me, the name "Coats" came with both honor and expectations. My grandfather, Dr. Joseph C. Coats, Sr., built a legacy of integrity, leadership, and faithfulness.

His name opened doors for me, often garnering respect before I even entered a room. But that same name also brought an unspoken pressure: to live up to his reputation, honor his legacy, and avoid tarnishing what he had built.

The Power of Favor

This past year, I was taking a seminary course with my mentor professor. Before each session, we would discuss how our week had gone and share any prayer requests. I was especially blessed because my grandfather had mentored this professor, and now he was mentoring me.

We began reminiscing about the past, noticing our similar upbringings; he, too, had parents who faithfully served in ministry.

In one of our sessions, we talked about how our lives parallel each other in the miraculous things we've both experienced. Doors have opened for us in ways that defy logic, and we've often wondered why God blessed us in such a manner and not others. The only conclusion we could reach was that God promises to bless the seed of those who have been faithful. When I consider this aspect of God's promises, I realize that some of the places and spaces where I personally thrive are directly connected to promises my grandfather never fully saw realized.

The passage my professor shared with me was Deuteronomy 6:10–12, which speaks of inheriting "houses full of all good things that you did not fill, and cisterns that you did not dig, and vineyards and olive trees that you did not plant—and when you eat and are full." It describes a time when God's providential care for Israel was evident, even though they had done nothing to deserve it.

Not only is there power in the meaning of a name, but that same name may be attached to favor through the faithfulness of a preceding generation.

A Name That Defines Identity

A name is more than a label—it can define identity. When people hear your name, they form a mental image of who you are based on your reputation and actions. This is why King Solomon, in his vast wisdom, declared that a good name is more valuable than great riches. Riches fade, but a name carries on.

The weight of a good name is a double-edged sword. On one hand, it offers opportunities and establishes credibility. On the other, it can feel like a burden, especially when others' expectations do not align with your personal journey. For years, I wrestled with the dual reality of carrying a "good name." It provided me with a platform, but also subjected me to relentless scrutiny.

Every misstep was magnified, not because of who I was, but because of the name I bore.

Biblical Perspective on Names

The Bible emphasizes the value of a good name repeatedly, yet it also reminds us that our ultimate identity is found in Christ. The Apostle Paul wrote in Galatians 2:20, *"It is no longer I who live, but Christ who lives in me."* This truth is liberating. No matter the name we carry or what legacy is attached to it, our worth and identity are rooted in our relationship with God.

God Himself places great importance on names. He reveals His character through names like **Jehovah Jireh** (The Lord Will Provide) and **EL Shaddai** (God Almighty).

When we consider that we are made in His image, it's no surprise that our names hold such weight.

Names in Today's World

I found out late in life that my Uncle Joe was the one who named me. Uncle Joe is the eldest son of Joseph Coats Sr. and essentially acted as a surrogate dad when I was growing up at my grandfather's house with my aunts and uncles.

I was the burden my uncle had of hanging out and caring for this young kid while my grandfather served in ministry. During that time, *"Little Pat"* would be everywhere Uncle Joe went. Many people thought I was his son.

One day, I asked my Uncle Joe who had given me my middle name. I'd been confused for a while because my full name is *Patrick Demetric Coats*, and I wondered who came up with the bright idea for "Demetric." True to form, Uncle Joe said, "I named you." His reason? *Demetric* rhymed with *Patrick*—that's all he could come up with. And so, there you have it: that's my name.

In modern culture, the significance of names hasn't diminished, even if the context has shifted.

The evolution of modern-day names is quite fascinating. Names like *plant, sky, storm, blue*, and *pink*, to name a few, may seem eclectic, yet we live in an age of personal branding where names are synonymous with reputation and influence. A name can open doors or close them. It can invoke respect, disdain, or indifference. In such a world, the pressure to protect and elevate one's name can be overwhelming.

For those of us who bear names with strong legacies—whether from family, faith, or other sources—the challenge is navigating the expectations attached to those names without losing sight of our true identity. The greatest lesson I've learned is that while the world may judge us by our names, God sees beyond them.

He sees our hearts, our potential, and our willingness to align our lives with His purpose.

Names are a Foundation, Not a Prison

A name is a gift, but it's also a responsibility. Whether your name is one of honor or a burden, it does not have to define your limitations. The beauty of God's design is that He can redeem and redefine any name. According to Scripture, Saul the persecutor became Paul the Apostle, and Simon the impulsive fisherman became Peter, the rock on which Christ would build His Church.

In the same way, God can use our names—whether they are celebrated or scorned—to fulfill His purposes. As I've discovered through my journey, a name is just the beginning. What truly matters is the life we live in response to that name and the identity we embrace in Christ.

What's in a name? More than we often realize. But even more important than the name we're given is the legacy we create—and the identity we claim—in Christ.

CHAPTER THREE

A Name is Connected to a Life Story

> *"But now, thus says the Lord, who created you, O Jacob, and He who formed you, O Israel: 'Fear not, for I have redeemed you; I have called you by your name; You are Mine.'" – Isaiah 43:1 (NKJV)*

Our names are often the starting point of our stories. They connect us to our origins, our families, and our heritage. Yet, for many, a name can feel like both a compass and a cage. It can point us toward a destiny while also confining us to the expectations and narratives of others. My journey has taught me that, while a name is significant, our true identity lies not in the label we bear but in the story, God is writing through us.

The Layers of a Name

Every name carries layers of meaning. Some are chosen with intention, symbolizing hope, faith, or heritage. Others are given out of tradition, convenience, or simply at random.

Regardless of the reasons, a name quickly becomes intertwined with a person's story, shaping how others perceive them—and how they perceive themselves.

For me, the name *"Coats"* was more than just a surname; it was a mantle. My grandfather, Dr. Joseph C. Coats, Sr., lived a life of exemplary faith, leadership, and service. His name was synonymous with integrity, love, and devotion to God's work.

While this legacy was a tremendous blessing, it also cast a shadow. From a young age, I was aware that people saw the name *"Coats"* before they saw me.

There are many layers to carrying a significant name. On one hand, it opens doors and provides opportunities that might otherwise be out of reach. On the other hand, it sets a standard that can feel impossible to achieve. Growing up, I often felt torn between honoring the Coats legacy and forging my own path. I didn't want to disappoint those who associated the name with excellence, but I also didn't want to lose myself in the process.

The Great Question

During my freshman year in college, my humanities professor asked a question on the first day of class that would stick with me for the rest of my life: "What do you want to be known for?" This question was so profound because, before that moment, it had never occurred to me that I possessed the power to define my own life. Up until then, everything had seemed predetermined or scripted. I was raised to go with the flow and trust that things would work out. It was as if my eyes were suddenly opened to possibilities—and also to the responsibilities of adulthood. Everything I do as an adult defines who I am, and **I** get to write the story. I can dream, I can try new things, and I can face the unknown world with limitless possibilities.

We are many things to many different people. To our siblings, we are brother or sister. To our spouse, we may be husband, wife, or friend.

To our children, we are Dad, Mom, or Coach. To our colleagues, we might be boss, coworker, teacher, or mentor.

While we relate to people in various ways, in every complex relational context, we are still our own person. We cannot escape our true selves. The more time others spend with us, the more they come to know who we really are.

Many of us have "nicknames" that only those in our closest, most intimate relationships use. A nickname often functions like a badge of honor, a term of endearment signaling that a relationship is deep and genuine—not superficial. Not everyone is afforded the liberty to call you by that special name. This privilege is generally reserved for those you love. I've been called "PC," "PDC," "Coats," "Rev," "Pastor," "Pastor Coach," "Babe," "Dad," "Big Bro," and "Baby Bro."

Each of these is used by a specific person or group in my life and carries a particular weight. Yet even being "all things to all people" comes with a significant burden.

While names carry many layers, one must first discover their true identity, which is found in Christ.

Rediscovering Identity in Christ

The greatest revelation of my life came when I discovered my true identity in Christ. It wasn't an overnight transformation but a journey—one of surrender to the Holy Spirit's transforming power in my life, unlearning brokenness, and relearning who I am in Christ. The pressure to live up to my family name had left me exhausted, striving to meet expectations that were often unspoken yet deeply felt. But when I began to understand that my worth wasn't tied to my respected last name but to **God's** love for me, everything changed.

The Bible is full of stories of people who found their true identity not in their earthly names but in their relationship with God. Consider Jacob. His name meant "supplanter" or "deceiver," reflecting his early life of trickery. But when he encountered God at Peniel, his name and identity changed. He became Israel, "one who struggles with God," a name that spoke to his transformation and purpose.

This truth became deeply personal for me. While I still honor the name "Coats" and the legacy it represents, I no longer see it as the foundation of my identity.

Instead, I view it as part of the larger story God is writing in my life. My identity is rooted in who I am as a beloved child of God, redeemed and called by Him.

Unlocking Promises and Possibilities

Understanding my identity in Christ unlocked promises and possibilities I never imagined. I had to give myself permission to embrace God's plans for my life without fearing failure or worrying about living up to my last name. When we see ourselves through **God's** eyes, we begin to understand the potential He has placed within us. I love the promise Apostle Paul wrote in Ephesians 3:20 — *"Now to him who is able to do far more abundantly than all that we ask or think, according to the power at work within us."* Be sure not to miss the latter, which shows that God's greater work in our lives flows from our surrender and our faith in His capacity to do big things.

The limitations of our earthly names—or the expectations of others—no longer bind us. Scripture is clear about the power of knowing who we are in Christ. In 1 Peter 2:9, we're described as *"a chosen generation, a royal priesthood, a holy nation, His own special people."* These words remind us that our value and purpose originate with God, not from any label the world might give us.

For years, I feared failing the "Coats" name. I worried that I or other family members might tarnish my grandfather's legacy or disappoint those who admired him. But as my faith matured, I realized that God's expectations for me far exceed the world's.

He isn't concerned with whether I meet the standard of a name; He cares about whether I fulfill the purposes **He** created me for.

Connecting the Dots

When we step back and view our lives through the lens of God's grace, we begin to see how every moment—every trial and every triumph—connects to His greater plan. Our names are part of that story, but they are not the whole story.

In my own life, I've seen countless instances of how God has used both the blessings and the challenges of bearing the Coats name to shape me into who I am today. The name gave me a foundation of faith and integrity, but it was through my personal struggles and encounters with God that I discovered my true identity.

For anyone wrestling with the weight of a name—whether it's one of honor or associated with pain—there is hope. **Your name is not your destiny.** Your identity is not confined to the labels others place on you. In Christ, you are a new creation. *"The old has passed away; behold, the new has come."* (2 Corinthians 5:17)

This powerful truth is liberating. It allows us to embrace the good in our names without being defined by the bad. It also enables us to honor our heritage while charting our own course.

Most importantly, it reminds us that our ultimate worth and identity come from the One who calls us by name and declares, "You are My beloved child."

As I reflect on my journey, I am grateful for the name "Coats" and the legacy it represents.

But I am even more thankful for **the name that is above every name—the name of Jesus.** In Him, I have found not only my identity but also my purpose, my peace, and my place in God's story.

What's in a name? A connection to a story. But when that story is written by the Author of life, the possibilities are endless.

CHAPTER FOUR

The Gatekeepers

> *"For the Lord does not see as man sees; for man looks at the outward appearance, but the Lord sees at the heart."'*
> *– 1 Samuel 16:7 (NKJV)*

Life often feels like a series of checkpoints guarded by *"gatekeepers"*—people or systems that determine who gains access to opportunities, recognition, and success. For many, these gatekeepers hold the power to validate or deny one's worth based on their perception of a name, reputation, or background. My journey has been filled with such gatekeepers, both literal and figurative, shaping my understanding of identity and purpose. Yet, through it all, I've come to realize that while people may judge us from the outside, **only God truly knows our potential**.

Navigating Family Traditions

Most families struggle with honoring the older generation while the younger one figures out its own path.

Growing up as a preacher's kid and witnessing behind-the-scenes church drama led me to believe, deep in my heart, that following in my grandfather's footsteps as a pastor was never something I wanted to do. I learned that church business can be messy, and people can be cruel. Yet, I couldn't escape God's call on my life; it happened suddenly as I grew up and became an adult.

When this happened, the "temperature" of my family dynamic shifted.

The "sweet little Pat" that everybody loved and got along with was now seen as a threat. As doors opened and I found success, I felt an unspoken pressure that I needed permission from the Coats elders (gatekeepers) before making any personal family moves.

Unbeknownst to me, there was a pecking order for who would thrive, who would be first, or who might hold certain positions in life.

What was perhaps misunderstood was the fact that it was in my heart to honor the Coats legacy but what was more important was to obey God's call on my life.

In retrospect, I realize my older family members had no ill will toward me. They were naturally trying to ensure that the Coats name was represented well by all who bore it.

In a family with such a great legacy, one must learn how to navigate the pressures of tradition in a way that honors the past but also pursues the future.

Gatekeepers in Society and Faith

Gatekeepers are everywhere. In the world of sports, it's often the coach or recruiter who decides who makes the team or gets playing time. In the workplace, it might be a manager or a decision-maker who determines promotions. Even in the church, gatekeepers exist, those who hold influence over who gets to lead or serve in various capacities.

Growing up as a *"Coats,"* I encountered gatekeepers who viewed me not as Patrick, but as "the grandson of Dr.

Joseph C. Coats, Sr." This connection opened some doors, but it also brought its own set of challenges.

People assumed that because of my family name, I had an unfair advantage, or worse, that I didn't need guidance or support. Others expected me to live up to my grandfather's legacy without recognizing the distinct path God was calling me to.

I saw this dynamic play out repeatedly—in school, on the playground, in church, and even in ministry. I often felt that people were more interested in the **name** I carried than in the **person** I was becoming.

It was as though I was sitting next to the coach, expected to earn my place simply by association.

The Transactional Nature of Gatekeepers

One of the hardest lessons I learned was that gatekeepers often operate on a transactional basis. In other words, they measure worth by what you can do for them or how well you align with their agenda. This kind of "love"—or rather, conditional approval—creates an environment where people are valued for their behavior rather than their God-given identity.

The story of David in the Bible illustrates this well. When the prophet Samuel came to anoint the next king of Israel, Jesse—David's father—presented all of his older, stronger, more impressive sons. David, the youngest and least likely candidate in his family's eyes, wasn't even invited to the lineup. Yet David was **God's** choice.

He wasn't the obvious pick, but he was the right one because God saw what others overlooked.

I've often felt like David in the field, underestimated and overlooked by the gatekeepers around me. But like David, I learned that **God's plan does not depend on human approval**. He calls and equips us for His purposes, regardless of who acknowledges it.

Living with Expectations

Gatekeepers aren't just people; they are also the expectations and assumptions tied to your name or role. In my case, the expectation was that I would follow in my grandfather's footsteps—both in ministry and in every other way. Although his legacy inspired me, the pressure to replicate it could be overwhelming.

I often wrestled with questions like:

- **How do I honor my grandfather's name while being true to myself?**
- **Can I meet others' expectations while pursuing God's unique calling for my life?**

This tension isn't unique to those with notable family names. It's something many people face in their careers, families, or communities.

The weight of these expectations can feel like a gatekeeper itself, standing between you and the life God has called you to live.

Breaking Through the Gates

What I've come to realize is that the only **gatekeeper** who truly matters is God.

In John 10:9, Jesus says, *"I am the gate; whoever enters through me will be saved."*

This powerful truth reframed my perspective. The world's gatekeepers may hold temporary authority, but ultimate access comes from God alone.

When I shifted my focus from pleasing people to seeking God's approval, I found the freedom I had longed for. I no longer needed to prove myself to others or strive to meet unrealistic expectations. Instead, I could rest in the assurance that God **saw** me, **knew** me, and had a plan for my life. This change in mindset didn't happen overnight. It took years of prayer, devotion, reflection, and learning to trust God's timing and direction. But once I embraced this truth, I began to see opportunities and relationships in a whole new light. The opinions of gatekeepers no longer defined me; God's purpose did.

A Word of Encouragement

To anyone who feels trapped by the gatekeepers in your life, I want to encourage you with this: **God's plan for you is not limited by human approval.** He sees your heart, He knows your potential, and He will reward your faithfulness. While others may look at outward appearances or judge you based on your name, God is writing a story far greater than anything the world can imagine.

Remember the words of Isaiah 43:19

"See, I am doing a new thing! Now it springs up; do you not perceive it? I am making a way in the wilderness and streams in the wasteland."

God is the ultimate Way Maker, and He can open doors no one else can shut.

Gatekeepers will always exist, but they don't have to control your story.

Whether they open doors for you or try to keep them closed, their power is limited. The true Author of your story is God, and **He** is the One who determines your path.

As I look back on my journey, I'm grateful for the lessons I've learned from the gatekeepers in my life. They taught me resilience, faith, and the importance of seeking God above all else. And while their influence may have shaped certain chapters of my story, it is God who **holds the pen**. The next time you encounter a gatekeeper—be it a person, an expectation, or a system—remember this: **your identity and purpose are not determined by them.** They are determined by the One who calls you by name and declares, "You are Mine."

CHAPTER FIVE

The Curse

> *"For I know the plans I have for you, declares the Lord, plans for welfare and not for evil, to give you a future and a hope."*
> *– Jeremiah 29:11 (NKJV)*

While a good name is a treasure, it can also be a weight. The *"curse"* of a good name isn't something often discussed, but it is real. Undoubtedly, many of you who picked up this book might suggest a different title. The word "curse" is strong, direct, and carries a negative connotation. Yet, the point of this book is to acknowledge that although the word "curse" may seem like hyperbole in this context, those who struggle with their name often feel that a **good** name can indeed feel like a curse. They are the voiceless who walk through life trying to find purpose, surrounded by few who can relate to their burden. In that sense, the "curse" lies in being misunderstood, in the impossibility of meeting others' high expectations, and in the pressure to remain true to oneself while doing so.

It's the unspoken side of success, legacy, and reputation—an experience many feel deeply but few discuss openly.

The Burden of Misunderstanding

One of the most challenging aspects of carrying a good name is simply being **understood**. People often project their ideas, assumptions, and even aspirations onto you because of your name. For me, being a "Coats" meant people had preconceived notions of who I should be, what I should say, how I should act, and even how I should think.

It often felt like living under a microscope, where every word and action was scrutinized.

It's a devastating reality to exist under the presumptions of someone else's vision for your life—particularly when that vision is disconnected from God's plan.

For years, I wrestled with questions like:

- *Am I allowed to make mistakes, or will they tarnish the Coats' legacy?*
- *How do I balance honoring my grandfather's name while pursuing my own calling?*

- *Will people ever see me for who I truly am, or will I always be defined by my name?*

This struggle reminded me of King David. As a young man, David was anointed by Samuel to be king, but he wasn't immediately understood, embraced, or accepted. Even his brothers misunderstood his motives when he brought food to the battlefield (1 Samuel 17:28).

David's story shows us that being chosen by God does not always guarantee being understood by others.

The Weight of Expectations

Expectations can be a double-edged sword. On one hand, they push you to strive for excellence. On the other, they can become an unbearable weight, especially when they are unrealistic or unattainable. Growing up, the expectations tied to the Coats name were clear:

- *Be a model of integrity.*
- *Succeed in everything you do.*
- *Avoid mistakes at all costs.*
- *Seek to become a Minister.*

These expectations weren't explicitly stated, but they were deeply felt. They came from well-meaning people who admired my grandfather's legacy and wanted to see it continue.

Yet, their good intentions often left me feeling like I was running a race I could never win.

The Bible is filled with stories of people who faced immense expectations. Moses, for example, was expected to lead the Israelites out of Egypt and into the Promised Land. Despite his faith and obedience, the weight of those expectations often left him frustrated and overwhelmed. In Numbers 20, we see Moses, in a moment of disobedience to God, striking the rock out of anger—a human weakness under the weight of leadership.

This single moment of weakness caused Moses to miss the Promised Land, though it did not remove God's care or loving presence from his life.

Isolation of the Pedestal

Another aspect of the curse is the isolation that comes with being placed on a pedestal. When people hold you in high regard, they sometimes forget that you are a fallen human. They may expect you always to have the right answers, never struggle, and consistently live up to their idealized view of you. The pedestal can be a lonely place. It's hard to share your struggles when people assume you have it all together. It's hard to ask for help when you're supposed to be the one offering it. And it's difficult to show vulnerability when others see it as a weakness rather than a strength. It's no wonder so many "PKs" (preacher's kids) struggle in life and leave the church.

Even Jesus experienced this. As He entered Jerusalem on a donkey, the crowds praised Him, shouting, "Hosanna!" (Matthew 21:9). Yet, just days later, many of those same people cried, "Crucify Him!" (Matthew 27:22).

Jesus understood the fickle nature of human expectations, facing the ultimate isolation when He hung on the cross, abandoned by many who had once followed him.

Finding Freedom in God's Grace

The turning point for me came when I realized I didn't have to carry the weight of expectations alone. God's grace is sufficient, even for those who bear the burden of a good name. His grace reminds us that we are not defined by people's opinions or expectations, but rather by His love, tender mercies, and grace He places on our lives. In 2 Corinthians 12:9, Paul writes, *"But he said to me, 'My grace is sufficient for you, for my power is made perfect in weakness.'"* This verse became a lifeline for me.

It reminded me that I didn't have to be perfect to honor the Coats' name or to fulfill God's calling. I simply had to be faithful and trust in His strength.

God's grace also frees us from the need to prove ourselves.

When we understand that our identity is rooted in Christ, we can let go of the fear of failure and embrace the freedom to be ourselves. We can honor the legacy of a good name without being enslaved by it.

Redeeming the Curse

The "curse" of a good name doesn't have to define us. With God's help, we can redeem it. We can turn the weight of expectations into a platform for testimony. We can transform misunderstandings into opportunities for growth. And we can use the pedestal not as a place of isolation but as a vantage point to point others toward Christ.

The story of Joseph is a powerful example. Betrayed by his brothers, sold into slavery, and falsely accused, Joseph could have been consumed by bitterness. Instead, he trusted in God's work and plan for his life. In Genesis 50:20, he tells his brothers, *"As for you, you meant evil against me, but God meant it for good."* Joseph's story shows us that God can take even the most challenging circumstances and use them for His glory.

Embracing the Journey

The "curse" of a good name is real, but it is not insurmountable. It's a reminder that life isn't always easy, even for those who seem to have it all. Yet it also reminds us of God's faithfulness. He sees our struggles, knows our concerns, understands our pain, and walks with us every step of the way.

As I reflect on my journey, I'm grateful for the lessons I've learned through the challenges of carrying a good name—lessons that have deepened my faith, strengthened my character, and drawn me closer to God.

For anyone struggling with the weight of expectations, the fear of failure, or simply wanting to be understood, know this: you are not alone. God sees you, knows your heart, and has a plan for your life that exceeds anything you could imagine. Trust Him and let Him turn your curse into a blessing.

CHAPTER SIX

Overcoming Generational Curses

> *"Christ redeemed us from the curse of the law by becoming a curse for us, for it is written, 'Cursed is everyone who is hanged on a tree."*
> *– Galatians 3:13 (NKJV)*

When we talk about curses, we often fail to realize that there are many **generational afflictions** we bear that can be handed down from generation to generation when left unaddressed. For some, a generational curse may be a predisposition to addiction, failure to love, poor parenting, toxic relationship issues, or other persistent struggles. By definition, **generational curses** are patterns of behaviors, sin, or hardship passed down from one generation to the next, which may feel like an inescapable weight.

These cycles may manifest in broken relationships, financial struggles, or even spiritual stagnation.

Overcoming these curses requires faith, intentionality, and reliance on God's power to break the chains of the past.

One fascinating perspective on **generational curses** arises from an episode of football Hall of Famer Cam Newton's "Fourth & One" podcast. The guest pastor suggested that a form of generational curse can be "living under the capacity" of your parents. This isn't meant to diminish what the previous generation achieved, but rather points to the idea that some children may be limited by the level of accomplishment they observed at home.

For example, if your parents did not attend college, you might never envision yourself pursuing higher education. While I'm not entirely certain I agree with this line of thought, it underscores how deeply we can be shaped by the generations that came before us.

Practical ways that may help break generational curses:

1. *Recognize the Curse*

The first step to overcoming a generational curse is identifying it. Acknowledge the patterns or struggles that have plagued your family history, whether they are relational, financial, emotional, or spiritual.

Being honest about these issues is not about assigning blame, but about bringing them into the light where God's healing can begin.

2. Confess and Renounce

Generational curses often persist in secrecy or denial. Confession breaks this cycle by acknowledging the sin or pattern before God. Renounce these curses in prayer, declaring that they no longer have authority over your life through the finished work of Jesus Christ. As 1 John 1:9 reminds us, *"If we confess our sins, He is faithful and just to forgive our sins and to cleanse us from all unrighteousness."*

3. Claim Your Identity in Christ

Generational Curses lose their power when we understand our identity in Christ. Jesus broke the power of sin and the curses tied to it through His death and resurrection. Galatians 3:13 assures us that Christ has redeemed us from the curse. Embrace this truth, reminding yourself daily that you are a new creation in Him (2 Corinthians 5:17).

4. Replace Old Patterns with Godly Habits

Breaking generational curses involves replacing destructive behaviors with godly habits. This might mean seeking professional counseling, setting boundaries, and cultivating spiritual disciplines like prayer, fasting, and studying God's Word. Intentional actions pave the way for lasting transformation.

5. Seek Community and Accountability

You don't have to overcome generational curses alone. Seek support from trusted family, friends, faith-filled community, or mentors who can pray with you, provide encouragement, and hold you accountable.

Ecclesiastes 4:12 reminds us, *"Though one may be overpowered, two can defend themselves. A cord with three strands is not quickly broken."*

6. Speak Life Over Future Generations

Breaking a generational curse doesn't end with you; it's about creating a new legacy. Speak blessings over your children and descendants, declaring God's promises for their lives. Deuteronomy 30:19-20 encourages us to *"choose life, so that you and your children may live."* Teach them to trust God and follow His ways, ensuring the cycle of freedom continues.

7. Trust God for Complete Redemption

Overcoming generational curses is a process, but God is faithful to complete the work He has begun in you. Trust Him to bring full redemption, healing, and restoration.

Remember, no curse is too strong for the power of God, and no family story is beyond His ability to rewrite. In Christ, generational curses can be transformed into generational blessings.

By trusting in His grace and walking in obedience, you can break the chains of the past and build a legacy of freedom, faith, and hope for generations.

You've Already Done the Work

One morning, my big brother John called me. We spoke almost every day, but this conversation was different— there was something heavy on his heart. He had been reflecting deeply on his family legacy and the name he carried. John and I share the same paternal father, Ronald Ferguson, but his story begins quite differently from mine.

At birth, John was left at the hospital and placed up for adoption. He grew up not knowing his biological mother or father, and this set him on a lifelong journey to discover his true family.

That journey became the foundation for John's compelling book, "*You May Not Be Who You Think You Are.*" In it, he chronicles his pursuit of his blood relatives, a riveting account of resilience, identity, and discovery.

54

John was named after John Isham Payne, a man who briefly dated his adoptive mother and stayed around long enough to ensure the adoption went through. Beyond that, there was no real connection—no fatherly bond.

John grew up carrying the name of a man who had simply done a favor for his adoptive mother, not a name steeped in personal attachment or legacy.

On this particular morning, John told me he had watched a documentary on family bloodlines.

It stirred something in him. After discovering and uniting with his biological siblings from our father's side, he was wrestling with the idea of changing his last name to Ferguson—our biological father's name. At 54 years old, he felt strongly about reclaiming this part of his identity. His reasoning was thoughtful and heartfelt. As he explained it to me, I listened carefully and compassionately. When he finished, I gently shared my perspective, hoping it would help him see the beauty of the name he already carried.

I told him, "John, even though you may not feel connected to the man whose name you bear, you've already done the work to make the name 'John I. Payne' your own.

Today, when people hear the name John Payne, they don't think of the man who signed adoption papers decades ago.

They think of you, my brother—the accomplished retired military officer, the devoted husband and father, the loving brother, and the loyal friend. They think of the incredible author who wrote his story with courage, and the civil servant who has risen to the pinnacle of leadership in his field."

I continued, "You've built that name. *John Isham Payne Jr.* isn't just a name; it's a legacy you've created. It's now *Dr. John I. Payne Jr.*, the man who recently earned his doctorate in education from the University of Miami—a name that represents perseverance, brilliance, and achievement. It's the name of a spiritual leader who guides his family in the ways of the Lord, a man who inspires his children to aim high, instilling in them a sense of purpose and a foundation for success.

Your name, John Payne is beautiful, and it holds profound meaning. To give it up for another name—one tied to broken family ties and generational struggles—would be to overlook the greatness of what God has done through you."

I reminded him of a truth we both hold dear: "God gave you that name." Everything that happens in our lives is 'so' ordered by God. The Apostle Paul affirms this principle in Romans 8:28, *And we know that all things work together for the good of those who love the Lord and are called according to His purposes."* "Big Bro," I said, "even though your beginning was rocky, God Carried you. Look at you now!

He turned what could have been generational curses into generational blessings. The name you were given wasn't an accident. God knew the path your life would take, and He knew how you would shape the name John Payne into something special."

We talked about how the Bible is full of examples of God giving new names. Abram became Abraham, Simon became Peter, and Jacob Became Israel. These names marked turning points in their lives and legacies. "John Payne doesn't disconnect you from your Ferguson bloodline," I said. "It enhances it. It is part of your testimony.

And now, you're charting a new legacy—a legacy built on faith, resilience, and the favor of God. Your name is not a limitation; it's a foundation."

I shared my own perspective. "For me, I could change my name to Patrick Ferguson," I said, "but God has already given me the name *Patrick D. Coats*—a name with a legacy I honor, and one I've been called to build upon. It's a name that allows me to chart a new course for my family, just as you're doing with yours."

As we wrapped up the conversation, I could hear peace settling into John's voice. He didn't need a new name to affirm his identity or his connection to his family. He had already done the work, and God had already redeemed the name he carried. *John I. Payne Jr.* wasn't just a name. It was a story, a legacy, and a gift—a reflection of the incredible man God had shaped him to be.

CHAPTER SEVEN

Reclaiming a Name

> *"Let us run with endurance the race that is set before us, looking to Jesus the founder and perfecter of our faith."*
> *–Hebrews 12:1-2 (NKJV)*

A name carries weight, legacy, expectations, and influence, but it is not the sum of who we are. At some point, we must decide whether we will allow our name to define us or reclaim it as part of a larger story. For me, reclaiming the name **Coats** meant surrendering to God's purpose and trusting that He could use my story—my struggles and my triumphs—to bring glory to Him.

The Beauty of the Relay Race

Life often looks like a relay race. Each generation runs its leg, passing the baton to the next.

The goal is to move the team forward, inching closer to the finish line, and to honor the efforts of those who have gone before us.

But as any runner knows, the race's success depends on each person running their "leg" with focus, endurance, and faithfulness. In a relay race, no single runner is responsible for the entire race. Each runner has a role to play, a distance to cover, and a time to hand off the baton. The same is true in life. We inherit the work, wisdom, and legacy of those who came before us, yet we are not bound to replicate their steps. Instead, our primary responsibility is to run **our** race faithfully, using the gifts and opportunities God has given us.

Reclaiming a name is like taking the baton in a relay race. It's about honoring the legacy of the past while embracing the unique path God has set before us. It's about recognizing that every leg of the race is significant, and that the ultimate goal is to fulfill God's purpose—not merely to meet human expectations.

Surrendering to Purpose

Reclaiming a name requires surrender—not to others' opinions, but to **God's** will.

It's about laying down our fears, doubts, and insecurities and trusting that God's plan is better than anything we could imagine. Surrender is synonymous with repentance. Repentance is more than acceptance of fortune; it is a turning away from our own ways and returning to God.

For years, I struggled with the pressure of living up to the Coats legacy. I wanted to honor my grandfather's name, but I also felt a deep yearning to carve out my own identity. It wasn't until I surrendered my ambitions to God that I found peace. That's when I realized my worth wasn't tied to others' expectations, but rather to the purpose God had placed on my life.

Surrendering doesn't mean giving up; it means letting go. It means releasing the need to control every aspect of our lives and trusting in God to guide us. As Proverbs 3:5–6 advises, *"Trust in the Lord with all your heart, and do not lean on your own understanding. In all your ways acknowledge Him, and He will make straight your paths."*

Running Your Leg of the Race

Reclaiming a name is not about erasing the past but redefining it. It involves taking the baton you've been handed and running **your** leg of the race with purpose and integrity. For me, this meant embracing the lessons of my upbringing while stepping into the unique calling God had placed on my life.

Each leg of the race is different. Some are smooth and straightforward, while others are filled with obstacles, challenges, and unexpected turns. Yet, no matter the terrain, the key is to **keep running**. As the writer of Hebrews encourages, we must run with endurance, fixing our eyes on Jesus, the founder and perfecter of our faith.

In my journey, running my leg of the race meant:

- **Embracing my identity in Christ:** Understanding that my worth is rooted in who I am as a child of God, not in the expectations of others.

- **Honoring the past while building the future:** Using the legacy of the Coats name as a foundation while pursuing God's unique purpose for my life.

- **Serving others:** Recognizing that my race is not about me but about advancing God's kingdom and impacting the lives of those around me.

The Power of Purpose

When we reclaim a name, we step into the power of **purpose**. We stop striving to meet human standards and begin living for God's glory. We let go of the fear of failure and embrace the freedom to be who God created us to be. The Apostle Paul understood the power of purpose.

He wrote in Philippians 3:13–14,

"Brothers and sisters, I do not consider myself yet to have taken hold of it. But one thing I do: Forgetting what is behind and straining toward what is ahead, I press on toward the goal to win the prize for which God has called me heavenward in Christ Jesus."

Reclaiming a name is about **pressing on**. It's about moving forward in faith, determination, and hope. It's about trusting that God can use every part of our story— the good, the bad, and the ugly— for His purposes.

Passing the Baton

One of the most beautiful aspects of the relay race is the handoff. As we run our leg of the race, we have the opportunity to pass the baton to the next generation.

This is not a burden but a **blessing**—an opportunity to pour into others, invest in their growth, and equip them for their own journey.

For me, passing the baton involves teaching and modeling for my children the values of **faith**, **integrity**, and **perseverance**. It means helping them understand the legacy of the Coats name while, more importantly, encouraging them to embrace their own identities in Christ. It means showing them that their worth is not tied to a name but to their relationship with the Lord. The **offer of Christ** to my children is my greatest deposit.

Reclaiming a name is not about taking control of your narrative; it's about aligning your story with God's grand plan. It's about recognizing that every name, every legacy, and every life has the potential to be redeemed for God's glory.

As I reflect on my journey, I'm reminded of Isaiah 61:3: *"To give them beauty for ashes, the oil of joy for mourning, the garment of praise for the spirit of heaviness; that they may be called trees of righteousness, the planting of the Lord, that He may be glorified."*

God has taken the ashes of my struggles and turned them into something beautiful. He has taken the weight of expectations and transformed it into the **joy of purpose**. To anyone wrestling with the legacy of a name, remember this: **your story is not over.** God is still writing it, and His plans for you are for good.

Run your race with endurance, reclaim your name with purpose, and trust that God will use your story to bless others and glorify Himself.

CHAPTER EIGHT

Charting a New Legacy

> *"Therefore if anyone is in Christ, he is a new creation;*
> *the old has passed away; behold the new has come."*
> *– 1 Corinthians 5:7 (ESV)*

Every legacy starts with a decision. Whether you inherit a legacy of greatness, pain, or something in between, you have the power to shape what it becomes for the next generation. **Charting a new legacy** is about taking the lessons of the past, embracing the identity you've found in Christ, and building a future that reflects God's purpose for your life. It's a journey marked by **faith, intention, and desire**.

A Name is a Starting Point, Not a Destination

Our names may connect us to a past, but they do not define our future. The beauty of life in Christ is that He gives us the freedom to break free from **generational cycles** and **human expectations**.

He allows us to carry forward what is good, **redeem** what is broken, and start anew where necessary.

For me, the **Coats** name came with both blessings and burdens. It stood for faith, integrity, and leadership, yet it also carried high expectations and pressures. Over time, I realized that **honoring** the Coats legacy didn't mean I had to be confined by it. Instead, I could build on its foundation while forging a path that reflected God's unique calling on my life. The Bible is full of individuals who **charted new legacies**. Abraham left his homeland to follow God's purpose, creating a legacy of faith that would span generations. Ruth, a Moabite widow, aligned herself with the God of Israel and became part of Christ's lineage.

These stories—and many others—remind us that **our past does not dictate our future**. Through God, we can create something new and beautiful.

Building with Intention

Charting a new legacy requires intentionality. It's not enough to simply hope for a brighter future; we must actively pursue it. This involves:

- **Defining your values:** What principles do you want to guide your life and legacy? For me, faith, family, integrity, and service are non-negotiables.

- **Setting clear goals:** What kind of impact do you want to have on your family, community, and the world? What do you want to be known for?

- **Breaking negative cycles:** Identify patterns or habits that need to change or die and commit to doing the hard work of transformation.

- **Investing in others:** A legacy is not just about what you achieve; it's about how you pour into the lives of others, especially the next generation.

As I've navigated this process, I've found that small, consistent steps make the biggest difference. Whether it's teaching my children biblical truths, serving in ministry, or modeling Christ-like behavior, every action contributes to the legacy I am building. Remember more is caught than taught.

Embracing the Challenges

Charting a new legacy is not without its challenges. There will be moments of doubt, setbacks, and resistance—both from within and from external forces. Paul writes in Ephesians 6:12:

"For we do not wrestle against flesh and blood, but against the rulers, against the authorities, against the cosmic powers over this present darkness, against the spiritual forces of evil in the heavenly places."

Understanding where the true battle lies is paramount. A greater perspective emerges when we discern that these challenges can deepen our faith and dependence on God.

One of the biggest challenges I've faced is the fear of not trying. Carrying the "Coats" name can be overwhelming at times, especially when I consider others' expectations. But I've learned to shift my focus from pleasing people to pleasing God. When I root my efforts in *His* strength rather than my own, I find peace and confidence.

Another challenge is the pressure to conform—the temptation to replicate someone else's path instead of following God's unique plan for your life. But our God is the One who makes our paths straight.

Leaving a Lasting Impact

A legacy isn't just about what you leave behind; it's about the ripple effects of your life on others. It's about inspiring those around you to live with purpose, courage, and faith. For me, this means investing in my family, church, and community in ways that continually point them to Christ.

One of the most humbling aspects of this journey is recognizing that my legacy is not mine alone—it's part of God's larger story. When I surrender my plans to Him, He takes what I offer and multiplies it beyond anything I could imagine. The Apostle Paul understood this well. In 1 Corinthians 3:6–7, he wrote:

"I planted, Apollos watered, but God gave the growth. So neither he who plants nor he who waters is anything, but only God who gives the growth."

This perspective reminds us that, while we are called to be faithful stewards, the ultimate outcome rests in God's hands.

As I look to the future, I am deeply aware of the privilege and the tremendous responsibility of passing the baton to the next generation.

It's not merely about transferring knowledge or resources; it's about equipping them with the faith and tools they need to run their own race.

For my beloved children, this means teaching them to root their identity in Christ rather than the Coats name. It means showing them that their worth comes from who they are in God's eyes, not from what they accomplish or how others perceive them. It means encouraging them to dream boldly, live faithfully, and serve wholeheartedly.

A Legacy for God's Glory

Charting a new legacy is not about seeking personal recognition, building a brand, or personal empire. It's about glorifying God and advancing His kingdom purposes.

It's about living a life of faith, reflecting His love, grace, and perfect will. When I look back on my life, I'm filled with gratitude for how God has guided, challenged, corrected, and redeemed me. The legacy I'm building is not perfect, but it is rooted in His perfect love. And that, more than anything, is what I hope to pass on.

To anyone reading this, I encourage you to take heart. Whether you're bearing the weight of a good name, overcoming the burden of a broken one, or starting fresh, know that God is with you. He has a plan for your life that exceeds anything you could imagine. Trust Him, and let Him guide you as you chart a legacy that brings glory to His name.

Your story is still unfolding, and the best is yet to come. Keep running your race, keep trusting in God, and keep building a legacy that will echo into eternity.

NOTES

www.ingramcontent.com/pod-product-compliance
Lightning Source LLC
Chambersburg PA
CBHW020414150626
46554CB00013B/948